THE JUNGLE POEMS OF LE CONTE DE LISLE

THE JUNGLE POEMS

OF

LE CONTE DE LISLE

translated by

DAVID R. SLAVITT

newamericanpress

Milwaukee, Wisconsin

n e w a m e r i c a n p r e s s

www.NewAmericanPress.com

Printed in the United States of America

ISBN 978-1-941561-08-9

Book design by David Bowen

Cover image © Andrei Kukla

For ordering information, please contact:
Ingram Book Group
One Ingram Blvd.
La Vergne, TN 37086
(800) 937-8000
orders@ingrambook.com

For Noah

TABLE OF CONTENTS

TRANSLATOR'S PREFACE

Charles-René Marie Leconte de Lisle was born on October 22, 1818, on the island of Réunion off the southeast coast of Africa. From that simple sentence, much of his oevre can be logically inferred. A fellow like that goes to France to complete his education, then in 1845 to Paris, where he finds himself among sophistication's feathery frou-frou. He witnesses the revolutions of 1848, bloody but unsuccessful rebellions by the Paris workers against a conservative turn in the politics of France. The gap between rich and poor was wider than it had been at any time since the Ancien Régime. Leconte de Lisle had grown up on his father's sugar plantation, which was operated by slaves. And he had a kind of disgust for what he saw around him in France, the artificiality and smugness whetting his appetite for the cliffs, beaches, and wildernesses of Réunion.

His friend Alphonse de Lamartine abandoned poetry for politics, but Leconte de Lisle thought this was distressingly wrong-headed. "The day when you will have made a beautiful work of art, you will have done more to prove your love of justice and right, than in writing twenty volumes of political economy," he wrote. "Let us give our lives for our political and social ideas; well and good; but let us not sacrifice our intelligence, which is far more valuable than life or death, for it is thanks to it that we shall shake from our feet the dust of this miserable earth and its passions, for the splendors of spiritual life."

The failure of the utopian socialist ideas in 1848 left him with a pessimism in which that art-for-art's-sake position seemed all the more practical, sensible, and modest. His poetry was called "Parnassian" which was as much an insult as a description. Readers of his time thought he was cold, unemotional, fussy, and aloof. Compared to Victor Hugo, he surely was. (He succeeded Hugo's chair as a member of the Académie Française.) It is Leconte de

Lisle's restraint that speaks to us now, his economy, and, I think, his trust in his readers. He does not beat us about the head and shoulders telling us what to feel. He just gives us the image and invites us to collaborate with him and find the right emotion that he has clearly enough implied.

To look at Leconte de Lisle now is to discover a sensibility strikingly similar to that of Elizabeth Bishop (with Africa instead of Brazil as his *mise en scène*). In some ways, he reminds me, too, of Wallace Stevens, stuck up in the fog of Hartford and longing for the glare of the tropics ("Home from Guatemala, back at the Waldorf"). He was an accomplished classicist who translated Homer's *Iliad* and Aschylus' "Eumenides." But it is as a poet that he fascinates me, and particularly as one whose technical abilities are impressive and whose subjects were often deliberately exotic and *primitif.* They are, in their way, pastorals of an odd kind. Most of the pieces I have translated and offer here are from his *Poèmes Barbares* although I have included a piece or two from other volumes. For that reason, and for the sake of clarity, I decided on *Jungle Poems*, which isn't far off.

If the French had certain reservations about their poet, the English were more enthusiastic. Edmond Gosse said of him:

…there is no French poet of our day more worthy of the attention of a serious English student. Leconte de Lisle cultivated the art of poetry with the most strenuous dignity and impersonality. He had a great reverence for the French language, and not a little of the zeal of the classic writers of the seventeenth century who aimed at the technical perfection of literature. He is lucid and direct almost beyond parallel. In England, among those who approach French literature with more enthusiasm than judgment, there is a tendency to plunge at once into what is fashionable for the moment on the Boulevard Saint Michel. We have seen British girls and boys affecting to appreciate Verlaine, and even Mallarmé, without having the smallest acquaintance

with Racine or Alfred de Vigny. It is pure *snobisme* to pretend
to admire [Mallarmé's] "Prose pour Des Esseintes" when
you are unable to construe Montaigne. For all such foreign
folly, the rigorous versification, the pure and lucid language,
and the luminous fancy of Leconte de Lisle may be
recommended as a medicine.

Gosse was right on the *monnaie*, accurate in his judgment, and
elegant in the elevation of his eyebrow as he pointed out a valuable
poet who had suffered from the modishness, not just of the French,
I'd say, but of the lit-biz in general.

DAVID R. SLAVITT
CAMBRIDGE, MASS.

LE SOMMEIL DU CONDOR

Par delà l'escalier des roides Cordillères,
par delà les brouillards hantés des aigles noirs,
plus haut que les sommets creusés en entonnoirs
où bout le flux sanglant des laves familières,
l'envergure pendante et rouge par endroits,
le vaste oiseau, tout plein d'une morne indolence,
regarde l'Amérique et l'espace en silence,
et le sombre soleil qui meurt dans ses yeux froids.
La nuit roule de l'est, où les pampas sauvages
sous les monts étagés s'élargissent sans fin;
elle endort le Chili, les villes, les rivages,
et la mer Pacifique et l'horizon divin;
du continent muet elle s'est emparée:
des sables aux coteaux, des gorges aux versants,
de cime en cime, elle enfle, en tourbillons croissants,
le lourd débordement de sa haute marée.
Lui, comme un spectre, seul, au front du pic altier,
baigné d'une lueur qui saigne sur la neige,
il attend cette mer sinistre qui l'assiège:
elle arrive, déferle, et le couvre en entier.

THE SLEEP OF THE CONDOR

Beyond the cold impervious heights of the Andes,
beyond the ghostly fogs in which the black
eagles nest, but higher, he circles back
and forth above the lava runnels. On these
huge wings, touched with red, lazily soaring
the enormous indolent condor glides and flies,
glaring down at empty space with eyes
indifferent—or even sullen—at the boring
continent stretched out below in space.
Those glittering eyes reflect the sun as it sets
and night rolls in from the east. The darkness lets
the savage pampas huddled under the face
of sheer cliffs disappear. Now Chile sleeps.
The cities and towns of its coastline, from this height,
dwindle to dreams of themselves in the fading light.
The featureless Pacific Ocean sweeps
away to that horizon of the mind
that even heaven can hardly comprehend.
Blackness engulfs the landscape to extend
from sand to the ever higher hills, behind
which are the lofty mountaintops. The tide
of darkness rises inexorably; it seeks
a shred of red still visible on the peaks
where it seems the ice has been wounded and has died.

Dans l'abîme sans fond la croix australe allume
sur les côtes du ciel son phare constellé.
Il râle de plaisir, il agite sa plume,
il érige son cou musculeux et pelé,
il s'enlève en fouettant l'âpre neige des Andes,
dans un cri rauque il monte où n'atteint pas le vent,
et, loin du globe noir, loin de l'astre vivant,
il dort dans l'air glacé, les ailes toutes grandes.

Still rising, it nears the lone and spectral bird
that almost disappears except for the glint
of the Southern Cross that offers at least a hint
of motion somewhere up there. Undeterred,
he screams in delight, swoops and soars, and stirs
the snow into wraith-like puffs that soon subside
before he climbs even higher for his ride
in the cold and emptiness that he prefers.
Below him a busy planet bustles. Its noise
does not come anywhere close to him in the air
and its primordial emptiness. Hanging there,
he dozes in an icy equipoise.

LE RÊVE DU JAGUAR

Sous les noirs acajous, les lianes en fleur,
Dans l'air lourd, immobile et saturé de mouches,
Pendent, et, s'enroulant en bas parmi les souches,
Bercent le perroquet splendide et querelleur,
L'araignée au dos jaune et les singes farouches.
C'est là que le tueur de boeufs et de chevaux,
Le long des vieux troncs morts à l'écorce moussue,
Sinistre et fatigué, revient à pas égaux.
Il va, frottant ses reins musculeux qu'il bossue;
Et, du mufle béant par la soif alourdi,
Un souffle rauque et bref, d'une brusque secousse,
Trouble les grands lézards, chauds des feux de midi,
Dont la fuite étincelle à travers l'herbe rousse.
En un creux du bois sombre interdit au soleil
Il s'affaisse, allongé sur quelque roche plate;
D'un large coup de langue il se lustre la patte;
Il cligne ses yeux d'or hébétés de sommeil;
Et, dans l'illusion de ses forces inertes,
Faisant mouvoir sa queue et frissonner ses flancs,
Il rêve qu'au milieu des plantations vertes,
Il enfonce d'un bond ses ongles ruisselants
Dans la chair des taureaux effarés et beuglants.

THE JAGUAR'S DREAM

Under the black mahogany, vines in bloom
hang in the heavy, silent, fly-filled air
enlivened by cries of the bright-colored parrots there
and the howlings of monkeys from somewhere deep in the gloom,
as the tired killer of oxen returns to his lair
over the mossy fallen tree trunks where he
pauses to stretch his rippling muscles and yawn.
His fearsome mouth gapes wide in lethargy.
He is thirsty too. Large lizards, green and tan,
flee from the rocks on which they sunbathed as though
he might take notice of them. He passes by,
indifferent. The blink of his golden eyes is slow
and languid. Is he purring? Is it a sigh?
He stretches himself out upon a flat
rock and, with his powerful tongue, he licks
a paw, grooming himself. (He is a cat.)
His muscles quiver. His elegant long tail flicks.
Does he dream, perhaps, of some lush green plantation
in which he leaps and plunges again and again
his claws into flesh? In his savage imagination
what can he do but attack the beasts in their pen?

LA PANTHÈRE NOIRE

Une rose lueur s'épand par les nuées;
L'horizon se dentelle, à l'Est, d'un vif éclair;
Et le collier nocturne, en perles dénouées,
S'égrène et tombe dans la mer.

Toute une part du ciel se vêt de molles flammes
Qu'il agrafe à son faîte étincelant et bleu.
Un pan traîne et rougit l'émeraude des lames
D'une pluie aux gouttes de feu.

Des bambous éveillés où le vent bat des ailes,
Des letchis au fruit pourpre et des cannelliers
Pétille la rosée en gerbes d'étincelles,
Montent des bruits frais, par milliers.

Et des monts et des bois, des fleurs, des hautes mousses,
Dans l'air tiède et subtil, brusquement dilaté,
S'épanouit un flot d'odeurs fortes et douces,
Plein de fièvre et de volupté.

Par les sentiers perdus au creux des forêts vierges
Où l'herbe épaisse fume au soleil du matin;
Le long des cours d'eau vive encaissés dans leurs berges,
Sous de verts arceaux de rotin;

La reine de Java, la noire chasseresse,
Avec l'aube, revient au gîte où ses petits
Parmi les os luisants miaulent de détresse,
Les uns sous les autres blottis.

THE BLACK PANTHER

A pink glow suffuses the cumulus,
tricked out with a delicate fringe of lace at the far
horizon in the east. A spectacular
flash undoes night's necklace. Superfluous,

its pearls shatter and fall into the sea.
The sky's peignoir, fastened by the bright
clip at its top, modifies the light
to fleck the water's green. There appears to be

a rain of flakes of fire. Bamboo trees
rustle, and the purple leechee fruit
dazzles in the dew in absolute
voluptuousness that cannot fail to please

the most demanding connoisseur. From the wood
there comes a rich mélange of sweet perfumes
we cannot find in any drawing rooms.
Nature here seems luxurious and good.

Tangled grasses steam in the morning heat
of the virgin forest in which, half-hidden, run
paths no man has ever walked upon
that were made by the quiet passage of animal feet.

Comes then the Queen of Java, the huntress, black
and sleek, returning to feed her small cubs where
they play among gnawed bones. She drags to her lair
what's left of the deer she has killed and is bringing back.

Inquiète, les yeux aigus comme des flèches,
Elle ondule, épiant l'ombre des rameaux lourds.
Quelques taches de sang, éparses, toutes fraîches,
Mouillent sa robe de velours.

Elle traîne après elle un reste de sa chasse,
Un quartier du beau cerf qu'elle a mangé la nuit;
Et sur la mousse en fleur une effroyable trace
Rouge, et chaude encore, la suit.

Autour, les papillons et les fauves abeilles
Effleurent à l'envi son dos souple du vol;
Les feuillages joyeux, de leurs mille corbeilles;
Sur ses pas parfument le sol.

Le python, du milieu d'un cactus écarlate,
Déroule son écaille, et, curieux témoin,
Par-dessus les buissons dressant sa tête plate,
La regarde passer de loin.

Sous la haute fougère elle glisse en silence,
Parmi les troncs moussus s'enfonce et disparaît.
Les bruits cessent, l'air brûle, et la lumière immense
Endort le ciel et la forêt.

She undulates along, and with her pale
yellow eyes peers into the underbrush
and the branches overhead. There is a hush
as she passes. The deer's blood leaves a crimson trail.

Butterflies dance above. Industrious bees
hover on their way to the flowers that grow
along the track to perfume the air. There is no
end to the dense forest's felicities,

except for the curious python that now rears
its flat head from a scarlet cactus bed
to watch the panther's progress with the dead
deer she drags until she disappears,

a dark phantom gliding into the deep
ferns and mossy tree-trunks. Gone from sight,
she leaves a changed silence beneath the bright
blue sky as if the forest were asleep.

LES JUNGLES

Sous l'herbe haute et sèche où le naja vermeil
Dans sa spirale d'or se déroule au soleil,
La bête formidable, habitante des jungles,
S'endort, le ventre en l'air, et dilate ses ongles.
De son mufle marbré qui s'ouvre, un souffle ardent
Fume; la langue rude et rose va pendant;
Et sur l'épais poitrail, chaud comme une fournaise,
Passe par intervalle un frémissement d'aise.
Toute rumeur s'éteint autour de son repos.
La panthère aux aguets rampe en arquant le dos;
Le python musculeux, aux écailles d'agate,
Sous les nopals aigus glisse sa tête plate;
Et dans l'air où son vol en cercle a flamboyé,
La cantharide vibre autour du roi rayé.
Lui, baigné par la flamme et remuant la queue,
Il dort tout un soleil sous l'immensité bleue.

Mais l'ombre en nappe noire à l'horizon descend,
La fraîcheur de la nuit a refroidi son sang;
Le vent passe au sommet des herbes ; il s'éveille,
Jette un morne regard au loin, et tend l'oreille.
Le désert est muet. Vers les cours d'eau cachés
Où fleurit le lotus sous les bambous penchés,
Il n'entend point bondir les daims aux jambes grêles,
Ni le troupeau léger des nocturnes gazelles.
Le frisson de la faim creuse son maigre flanc
Hérissé, sur soi-même il tourne en grommelant;
Contre le sol rugueux il s'étire et se traîne,
Flaire l'étroit sentier qui conduit à la plaine,
Et, se levant dans l'herbe avec un bâillement,
Au travers de la nuit miaule tristement.

JUNGLE

In the dry grass a vermeil cobra lolls
coiled in the golden sun, while a great beast sprawls
dozing nearby, supine, although with claws
extended. His eyes are closed and his huge jaws
gape so that his tongue protrudes His breath
is hot and shallow: his dreams must be of death.
His muscles quiver. Excitement and delight
possess him as if he were on the prowl at night.
A watchful panther stretches and arches its spine,
while a muscular banded python, in its malign
intent, slithers beneath the prickly pear
flicking its tongue repeatedly into the air.
Blister-beetles vibrate in their swarm
that the animal's tail disturbs but cannot harm.
Bathed in the sun's pleasant warmth for a few
hours he drowses under the sky's pale blue.

But black shadows lengthen and night comes on
with gentle winds that cool the blood. With a yawn
he wakes and looks around. He pricks an ear.
Although the desert is silent, he can hear
from the riverbank where the lotus flowers are floating
and bamboo rustles, another sound denoting
gazelles that make their way on dainty feet—
the night's invitation to easy, delicious meat.
He feels a pang of hunger, which is a thrilling
sensation that leads to the further excitement of killing.
He raises himself and slinks across rough ground
sniffing a path toward what his ears have found
and he creeps to the watering hole, barely stirring
the grass as makes his way, quietly purring.

LA MORT DU SOLEIL

Le vent d'automne, aux bruits lointains des mers pareil,
Plein d'adieux solennels, de plaintes inconnues,
Balance tristement le long des avenues
Les lourds massifs rougis de ton sang, ô soleil!

La feuille en tourbillons s'envole par les nues;
Et l'on voit osciller, dans un fleuve vermeil,
Aux approches du soir inclinés au sommeil,
De grands nids teints de pourpre au bout des branches nues.

Tombe, Astre glorieux, source et flambeau du jour!
Ta gloire en nappes d'or coule de ta blessure,
Comme d'un sein puissant tombe un suprême amour.

Meurs donc, tu renaîtras! L'espérance en est sûre.
Mais qui rendra la vie et la flamme et la voix
Au coeur qui s'est brisé pour la dernière fois?

DEATH OF THE SUN

The autumn wind's constant susurrus seems
like the sound of the sea beating upon the shore,
a whispered farewell, a commentary on your
steady blood-red descent and your last gleams.

The light changes, the river goes from vermeil
to niello as the landscape prepares for sleep.
Shadows of tree trunks elongate and creep
along the darkening grass at the end of day.

Fall, you heavenly body, the earth's flambeau!
The golden splendor flowing out of your wound
pours upon us more love than we can know.

Die, but know that you will be reborn soon.
Your hope is certain. But what man's heart survives,
not merely being broken but excised with knives?

LA CHUTE DES ÉTOILES

Tombez, ô perles dénouées,
Pâles étoiles, dans la mer.
Un brouillard de roses nuées
Émerge de l'horizon clair;
À l'Orient plein d'étincelles
Le vent joyeux bat de ses ailes
L'onde que brode un vif éclair.
Tombez, ô perles immortelles,
Pâles étoiles, dans la mer.

Plongez sous les écumes fraîches
De l'Océan mystérieux.
La lumière crible de flèches
Le faîte des monts radieux,
Mille et mille cris, par fusées,
Sortent des bois lourds de rosées;
Une musique vole aux cieux.
Plongez, de larmes arrosées,
Dans l'Océan mystérieux.

Fuyez, astres mélancoliques,
Ô Paradis lointains encor!
L'aurore aux lèvres métalliques
Rit dans le ciel et prend l'essor;
Elle se vêt de molles flammes,
Et sur l'émeraude des lames
Fait pétiller des gouttes d'or.
Fuyez, mondes où vont les âmes,
Ô Paradis lointains encor!

FALLING STARS

Like unstrung pearls,
the pale stars fall
into the sea.
A rose mist swirls.
The wind breathes free;
waves heave and stall
from the distant horizon. We
see these showers of sparks
as the pearls fall into the sea

and immerse themselves in the foam.
The mountaintops look on
as the stars at last reach home,
like music, there and gone.
We did not see them rise
but only their fall, a surprise,
from the heaven's empery
into the pitiless sea.

Enfants du paradis,
you leave such a brief trace
of your fall into the sea
from your distant domain
and put on a cheerful face.
You seem to celebrate
your metamorphosis
in your gold robes of state,
the end of your brief reign
as you enter the world below
and go where all souls go.

Allez, étoiles, aux nuits douces,
Aux cieux muets de l'Occident.
Sur les feuillages et les mousses
Le soleil darde un oeil ardent;
Les cerfs, par bonds, dans les vallées,
Se baignent aux sources troublées,
Le bruit des hommes va grondant.
Allez, ô blanches exilées,
Aux cieux muets de l'Occident.

Heureux qui vous suit, clartés mornes,
Ô lampes qui versez l'oubli!
Comme vous, dans l'ombre sans bornes,
Heureux qui roule enseveli!
Celui-là vers la paix s'élance:
Haine, amour, larmes, violence,
Ce qui fut l'homme est aboli.
Donnez-nous l'éternel silence,
Ô lampes qui versez l'oubli!

Go, then, on these warm nights
from the silences of the sky
flashing as you go by.
In daytime, the sun's eye
glares down at the deer
in the hills and valleys here
and the troubles of mankind
that nothing can mollify.
You take little notice of these
vicissitudes and are blind
to all but the vast sea's
welcome to your bright lights.

Those who follow the lead
of your sad lights that cease
when they reach their goal of peace
beyond love, hatred, and violence,
are fortunate indeed.
That fine celestial silence
you knew, you have found again
beneath the realm of men
in your spectacular fall
to nothing, nothing at all.

LA RAVINE SAINT-GILLES

La gorge est pleine d'ombre où, sous les bambous grêles,
Le soleil au zénith n'a jamais resplendi,
Où les filtrations des sources naturelles
S'unissent au silence enflammé de midi.

De la lave durcie aux fissures moussues,
Au travers des lichens l'eau tombe en ruisselant,
S'y perd, et, se creusant de soudaines issues,
Germe et circule au fond parmi le gravier blanc.

Un bassin aux reflets d'un bleu noir y repose,
Morne et glacé, tandis que, le long des blocs lourds,
La liane en treillis suspend sa cloche rose,
Entre d'épais gazons aux touffes de velours.

Sur les rebords saillants où le cactus éclate,
Errant des vétivers aux aloès fleuris,
Le cardinal, vêtu de sa plume écarlate,
En leurs nids cotonneux trouble les colibris.

Les martins au bec jaune et les vertes perruches,
Du haut des pics aigus, regardent l'eau dormir,
Et, dans un rayon vif, autour des noires ruches,
On entend un vol d'or tournoyer et frémir.

Soufflant leur vapeur chaude au-dessus des arbustes,
Suspendus au sentier d'herbe rude entravé,
Des bœufs de Tamatave, indolents et robustes,
Hument l'air du ravin que l'eau vive a lavé;

THE SAINT-GILLES RAVINE

The gorge is full of shadow, and under the tall
bamboo the sun never penetrates,
even at noon. The water's silent fall
from springs in the rocks only exaggerates

the stillness. In the hardened lava's cracks
are moss and lichens through which the waters pour,
forming a pattern of their erratic tracks
to the white gravel below on the gorge's floor

and the blue-black shimmering pools that intensify
the gloom of the place. Thick lianas cross
overhead with bell-like flowers. Nearby
velvety grasses thrust up through the moss

and here and there a cactus explodes into bloom
and the vetiver displays its banneret.
A scarlet cardinal's cottony nest on some
tree branch the hummingbirds view as a threat.

There are martins with bright yellow beaks and green
parakeets on the crags looking down at the still
water below. And one can hear the obscene
cackle of crows, repetitive and shrill.

Breathing puffs of vapor into the air,
the slow Madagascar cattle saunter through
the scrub on the narrow pathways they find there
on the floor of the ravine, and as they do

Et les grands papillons aux ailes magnifiques,
La rose sauterelle, en ses bonds familiers,
Sur leur bosse calleuse et leurs reins pacifiques
Sans peur du fouet velu se posent par milliers.

À la pente du roc que la flamme pénètre,
Le lézard souple et long s'enivre de sommeil,
Et, par instants, saisi d'un frisson de bien-être,
Il agite son dos d'émeraude au soleil.

Sous les réduits de mousse où les cailles replètes
De la chaude savane évitent les ardeurs,
Glissant sur le velours de leurs pattes discrètes
L'oeil mi-clos de désir, rampent les chats rôdeurs.

Et quelque Noir, assis sur un quartier de lave,
Gardien des bœufs épars paissant l'herbage amer,
Un haillon rouge aux reins, fredonne un air saklave,
Et songe à la grande Île en regardant la mer.

Ainsi, sur les deux bords de la gorge profonde,
Rayonne, chante et rêve, en un même moment,
Toute forme vivante et qui fourmille au monde
Mais formes, sons, couleurs, s'arrêtent brusquement.

Plus bas, tout est muet et noir au sein du gouffre,
Depuis que la montagne, en émergeant des flots,
Rugissante, et par jets de granit et de soufre,
Se figea dans le ciel et connut le repos.

À peine une échappée, étincelante et bleue,
Laisse-t-elle entrevoir, en un pan du ciel pur,
Vers Rodrigue ou Ceylan le vol des paille-en-queue,
Comme un flocon de neige égaré dans l'azur.

brightly colored butterflies execute slow
maneuvers as grasshoppers leap and settle
on the gentle animals' backs that do not know
the fear of the lash that torments other cattle.

On top of a rock where the sunlight penetrates
a lizard stretches out in the cool ravine
to enjoy the warmth. He rests and luxuriates
while the scales of his skin glisten an emerald green.

In little nooks in the moss the plump quail find
refuge from the hot savannah's heat,
although there are hungry cats that are inclined
to creep toward them on silent velvety feet.

A cowherd, a Negro, has found a place to sit
on a chunk of lava. He watches the herd and he
sports a red rag around his waist, a bit
of finery. He stares out at the sea

and hums, so that his songs and dreams combine
to fill the deep ravine. Here life abounds,
and yet in this isolation they refine
themselves to abstract colors, odors, and sounds.

Deeper in the abyss there has been silence
and darkness ever since the mountain arose
from the sea with jets of flame and a violence
that subsided as the volcano struck a pose.

One spot was spared, and here there is the blue
of sky and ocean, looking eastward on
Rodrigues Island and, beyond that, to Ceylon.
Sometimes a soaring straw-tail sails into view.

Hors ce point lumineux qui sur l'onde palpite,
La ravine s'endort dans l'immobile nuit;
Et quand un roc miné d'en haut s'y précipite,
Il n'éveille pas même un écho de son bruit.

Pour qui sait pénétrer, Nature, dans tes voies,
L'illusion t'enserre et ta surface ment:
Au fond de tes fureurs, comme au fond de tes joies,
Ta force est sans ivresse et sans emportement.

Tel, parmi les sanglots, les rires et les haines,
Heureux qui porte en soi, d'indifférence empli,
Un impassible cœur sourd aux rumeurs humaines,
Un gouffre inviolé de silence et d'oubli!

La vie a beau frémir autour de ce cœur morne,
Muet comme un ascète absorbé par son Dieu;
Tout roule sans écho dans son ombre sans borne,
Et rien n'y luit du ciel, hormis un trait de feu.

Mais ce peu de lumière à ce néant fidèle,
C'est le reflet perdu des espaces meilleurs!
C'est ton rapide éclair, Espérance éternelle,
Qui l'éveille en sa tombe et le convie ailleurs!

Waves beat on the cliffs and now and then
a rock will erode and fall but barely rouse
the sleepy valley, for silence reigns again,
the echo dies, and the gorge resumes its drowse.

Who can presume to understand Nature's ways?
Her illusions mislead, her surface is falsehood.
As indifferent to condemnation as to praise,
her immense powers are neither wicked nor good.

Learn from her to rise above tears and laughter,
love and hate. Study indifference that she
exemplifies, an ideal to strive after,
accepting what was, what is, and what will be.

One trembles at life's beauty. The mournful heart
is stricken dumb, imagining some higher
silent awe of which this is a part,
an empty sky with a single flash of fire.

But from this brief glimpse into nothingness
there comes the hint of a better world elsewhere
beyond the tomb, eternal, featureless
and we hope that we may be invited there.

LA FORÊT VIERGE

Depuis le jour antique où germa sa semence,
Cette forêt sans fin, aux feuillages houleux,
S'enfonce puissamment dans les horizons bleus
Comme une sombre mer qu'enfle un soupir immense.

Sur le sol convulsif l'homme n'était pas né
Qu'elle emplissait déjà, mille fois séculaire,
De son ombre, de son repos, de sa colère,
Un large pan du globe encore décharné.

Dans le vertigineux courant des heures brèves,
Du sein des grandes eaux, sous les cieux rayonnants,
Elle a vu tour à tour jaillir des continents
Et d'autres s'engloutir au loin, tels que des rêves.

Les étés flamboyants sur elle ont resplendi,
Les assauts furieux des vents l'ont secouée,
Et la foudre à ses troncs en lambeaux s'est nouée;
Mais en vain : l'indomptable a toujours reverdi.

Elle roule, emportant ses gorges, ses cavernes,
Ses blocs moussus, ses lacs hérissés et fumants
Où, par les mornes nuits, geignent les caïmans
Dans les roseaux bourbeux où luisent leurs yeux ternes;

Ses gorilles ventrus hurlant à pleine voix,
Ses éléphants gercés comme une vieille écorce,
Qui, rompant les halliers effondrés de leur force,
S'enivrent de l'horreur ineffable des bois;

THE VIRGIN FOREST

From the earliest days when small seeds first began
to sprout, this forest with all its storm-tossed trees
has stretched away to the blue horizon-like seas
in which the breakers crash upon the sand.

The meddlings of mankind had not yet
begun. The forest was thousands of centuries old.
Its moods of repose or anger as they took hold
were volatile with promise as well as threat.

In the steady rain of time's brief days and hours
that poured from heaven's bosom it saw immense
transformations as, on its continents,
winters gave way to springtime's leaves and flowers.

Blazing summers followed along, but then
came onslaughts of the furious winds that blow
down trees lightning has spared, and there was snow
and its blanket of denial, and spring again.

It seems, with its gorges, caves, hills that rise,
mossy boulders, and lakes covered with mist,
alive. In its darknesses, what beasts exist
along with the whining caimans with glowing eyes?

Its huge gorillas pound their chests and shriek.
Its elephants that have shaggy bark for skin
break through thickets and uproot large trees in
the indifference of strength to the havoc it may wreak.

Ses buffles au front plat, irritables et louches,
Enfouis dans la vase épaisse des grands trous,
Et ses lions rêveurs traînant leurs cheveux roux
Et balayant du fouet l'essaim strident des mouches;

Ses fleuves monstrueux, débordants, vagabonds,
Tombés des pics lointains, sans noms et sans rivages,
Qui versent brusquement leurs écumes sauvages
De gouffre en gouffre avec d'irrésistibles bonds.

Et des ravins, des rocs, de la fange, du sable,
Des arbres, des buissons, de l'herbe, incessamment
Se prolonge et s'accroît l'ancien rugissement
Qu'a toujours exhalé son sein impérissable.

Les siècles ont coulé, rien ne s'est épuisé,
Rien n'a jamais rompu sa vigueur immortelle;
Il faudrait, pour finir, que, trébuchant sous elle,
Le terre s'écroulât comme un vase brisé.

Ô forêt ! Ce vieux globe a bien des ans à vivre;
N'en attends point le terme et crains tout de demain,
Ô mère des lions, ta mort est en chemin,
Et la hache est au flanc de l'orgueil qui t'enivre.

Sur cette plage ardente où tes rudes massifs,
Courbant le dôme lourd de leur verdeur première,
Font de grands morceaux d'ombre entourés de lumière
Où méditent debout tes éléphants pensifs;

Comme une irruption de fourmis en voyage
Qu'on écrase et qu'on brûle et qui marchent toujours,
Les flots t'apporteront le roi des derniers jours,
Le destructeur des bois, l'homme au pâle visage.

Its water buffalo, irritable, lies
in his wallow hole half sunk in the black mud,
while the lazy lion, his paws still stained with blood,
sweeps the wisk of his tail at a swarm of flies.

Its enormous rivers meander randomly,
pouring from distant peaks that are yet to be named
and eddying white waters not yet tamed
that pour from lake to lake and into the sea,

rapid through rocky ravines, then wider and slow.
It devours bushes and towering trees it sweeps
along in its current, while its dull roaring keeps
up an unvarying continuo.

The centuries have flowed, nothing has decayed
or broken it in its immortal force;
that would require some defect in the source
of nature—for earth to fail like something man-made.

This ancient forest that has by now lived through
millennia has no fear of tomorrow.
But O mother of lions, with greatest sorrow,
I tell you the axe is now being honed for you.

On this scorching beach where your sand is packed hard
large angular pieces of shadow loom
of heavy equipment brought here for your doom.
The elephants gaze as if they were on guard.

Think of a line of ants going someplace
although some are crushed and some are burned but still
moving: so does time, as if with a will
of its own, bring you the man with the pale face

Il aura tant rongé, tari jusqu'à la fin
Le monde où pullulait sa race inassouvie,
Qu'à ta pleine mamelle où regorge la vie
Il se cramponnera dans sa soif et sa faim.

Il déracinera tes baobabs superbes,
Il creusera le lit de tes fleuves domptés;
Et tes plus forts enfants fuiront épouvantés
Devant ce vermisseau plus frêle que tes herbes.

Mieux que la foudre errant à travers tes fourrés,
Sa torche embrasera coteau, vallon et plaine;
Tu t'évanouiras au vent de son haleine;
Son œuvre grandira sur tes débris sacrés.

Plus de fracas sonore aux parois des abîmes;
Des rires, des bruits vils, des cris de désespoir.
Entre des murs hideux un fourmillement noir;
Plus d'arceaux de feuillage aux profondeurs sublimes.

Mais tu pourras dormir, vengée et sans regret,
Dans la profonde nuit où tout doit redescendre:
Les larmes et le sang arroseront ta cendre,
Et tu rejailliras de la nôtre, ô forêt!

who will come in his swarms to gnaw with an appetite
that nothing in this world can satisfy.
Your bounty on which so many creatures rely
he will arrogate to himself as if by right.

He will uproot your beautiful baobab trees;
he will dredge the beds of your rivers or dam them; he
will make even your strongest children flee,
although he is much more fragile than any of these.

Worse than random lightning that strikes you, he
will torch your hillsides, valleys, and wide plains,
imposing upon you not by strength but brains
to exploit whatever he can of your sacred debris.

I can hear the crashing noises from the abyss,
the drunken laughter, the shouts and cries of despair.
I can feel it deep in the ground and in the air.
And he will not even see what he takes as his.

But you can sleep in your great good night and know
neither regret nor thoughts of revenge: his tears
will water your ashes in not so many years,
expressing the grief you do not deign to show.

LE JAGUAR

Sous le rideau lointain des escarpements sombres
La lumière, par flots écumeux, semble choir;
Et les mornes pampas où s'allongent les ombres
Frémissent vaguement à la fraîcheur du soir.

Des marais hérissés d'herbes hautes et rudes,
Des sables, des massifs d'arbres, des rochers nus,
Montent, roulent, épars, du fond des solitudes,
De sinistres soupirs au soleil inconnus.

La lune, qui s'allume entre des vapeurs blanches,
Sur la vase d'un fleuve aux sourds bouillonnements,
Froide et dure, à travers l'épais réseau des branches,
Fait reluire le dos rugueux des caïmans.

Les uns, le long du bord traînant leurs cuisses torses,
Pleins de faim, font claquer leurs mâchoires de fer;
D'autres, tels que des troncs vêtus d'âpres écorces,
Gisent, entre-bâillant la gueule aux courants d'air.

Dans l'acajou fourchu, lové comme un reptile,
C'est l'heure où, l'oeil mi-clos et le mufle en avant,
Le chasseur au beau poil flaire une odeur subtile,
Un parfum de chair vive égaré dans le vent.

Ramassé sur ses reins musculeux, il dispose
Ses ongles et ses dents pour son oeuvre de mort;
Il se lisse la barbe avec sa langue rose;
Il laboure l'écorce et l'arrache et la mord.

THE JAGUAR

Below the high cliffs' beetling curtain wall
the light descends on the gentle waves on the strand.
Inland, in the pampas, shadows fall
and in the evening lengthen along the sand.

On the cat tails and tall grasses of the marsh,
on the clumps of little scrub trees, on the bare
rocks, solitude now declares its harsh
ukase sending the light of the sun elsewhere.

The moon appears and between white vapor's veils
shines on the cold muddy river to make
a jeweler's ornamentation on the scales
of the alligator's back and the water snake.

On his stubby twisted legs on the riverbank
the alligator opens his jaws; in disguise
as a sunken log another lies in the dank
mud with only his nostrils showing and eyes.

On a mahogany tree branch, high off the ground,
the jaguar crouches, his eyes half-closed, his hair
gorgeous. He sniffs the air, for he has found
a subtle odor of flesh that the wind brings there.

His teeth were made for just this work. With his tongue
he licks his whiskers. He stretches his legs to score
the bark and hone his claws as he makes the long
parallel lines that he has made before.

Tordant sa souple queue en spirale, il en fouette
Le tronc de l'acajou d'un brusque enroulement;
Puis sur sa patte roide il allonge la tête,
Et, comme pour dormir, il râle doucement.

Mais voici qu'il se tait, et, tel qu'un bloc de pierre,
Immobile, s'affaisse au milieu des rameaux:
Un grand boeuf des pampas entre dans la clairière,
Corne haute et deux jets de fumée aux naseaux.

Celui-ci fait trois pas. La peur le cloue en place:
Au sommet d'un tronc noir qu'il effleure en passant,
Plantés droit dans sa chair où court un froid de glace,
Flambent deux yeux zébrés d'or, d'agate et de sang.

Stupide, vacillant sur ses jambes inertes,
Il pousse contre terre un mugissement fou;
Et le jaguar, du creux des branches entr'ouvertes,
Se détend comme un arc et le saisit au cou.

Le boeuf cède, en trouant la terre de ses cornes,
Sous le choc imprévu qui le force à plier;
Mais bientôt, furieux, par les plaines sans bornes
Il emporte au hasard son fauve cavalier.

Sur le sable mouvant qui s'amoncelle en dune,
De marais, de rochers, de buissons entravé,
Ils passent, aux lueurs blafardes de la lune,
L'un ivre, aveugle, en sang, l'autre à sa chair rivé.

Ils plongent au plus noir de l'immobile espace,
Et l'horizon recule et s'élargit toujours;
Et, d'instants en instants, leur rumeur qui s'efface
Dans la nuit et la mort enfonce ses bruits sourds.

Rotating his tail in a spiral, he whips
the trunk of the tree a couple of times. He is stiff
from having been asleep. With his claws he grips
the branch as he stretches his neck for another sniff

and abruptly falls as silent as stone, for now,
wandering out of the pampas and under the tree
there comes the large and ungainly shape of a cow.
Or a bull, for with those horns it is a he.

The bull takes another step, then stops in fear
as its flank touches the tree trunk. From overhead
the jaguar pounces. It feels the sudden sear
of claws, and sees the eyes flame gold and red.

Stunned, stupid, staggering, his feet
collapse. It falls to the ground a roaring beast
that the jaguar already thinks is so much meat
as he seizes upon the neck of his ample feast.

The bull yields, plowing the earth with its horn,
having been vanquished by this sudden assault.
The jaguar is too busy to gloat or scorn,
too occupied with feeding to pause or halt.

The larger landscape is ghastly: beneath the dune
there is a swamp, and large black rocks in the clear
reddish light of a low, nearly full moon
are as drunk with blood as is the jaguar here.

Their kinship colors somehow all of this space
in which the horizon recedes vertiginously.
There is a palpable silence with hardly a trace
of deadened thuds from under the jaguar's tree.

L'ABOMA

Du pied des sommets bleus, là-bas, dans le ciel clair,
Épandu sur les lacs, les forêts et les plaines,
Le vaste fleuve, enflé de cent rivières pleines,
S'en va vers l'orient du monde et vers la mer.

L'or fluide du jour jaillit en gerbes vives,
Monte, s'épanouit, retombe, et, ruisselant
Comme un rose incendie au fleuve étincelant,
Semble le dilater au-dessus de ses rives.

Sous les palétuviers visqueux, aux longs arceaux,
Dans l'enchevêtrement aigu des herbes grasses,
Tourbillonne l'essaim des moustiques voraces
Et des mouches dont l'aile égratigne les eaux.

L'ara vêtu de pourpre éveille les reptiles,
Crotales et corails, agacés de ses cris,
Et qui bercent le nid grêle des colibris
Par l'ondulation de leurs fuites subtiles.

Au loin, à l'horizon des pacages herbeux,
Où la brume en flocons transparents s'évapore,
Passent, aiguillonnés des flèches de l'aurore,
Des troupeaux d'étalons sauvages et de boeufs.

Ils courent, les uns fiers et joyeux, l'oeil farouche,
Crins hérissés, la queue au vent, et par milliers
Martelant bonds sur bonds les déserts familiers,
Et ceux-ci, mufle en terre et la bave à la bouche.

THE ABOMA

At the foot of the distant peaks beneath the clear
sky the river spreads over lakes and plains
and into the forest, swollen with water that drains
from a hundred others and flows eastward from here

to the sea. The liquid gold of the day in gay
jets, rises, thrives, eddies and splashes.
Like a long pink fire that glows and flashes,
it widens its banks as it goes upon its way.

Under the mangrove's catenary vines
in the riotous tangle of variegated weeds
mosquitoes swarm, hungry for whatever bleeds,
and flies whose buzzing adds to their shrill whines.

The macaw, garbed in purple, rouses the snakes,
rattlers and coral, annoyed by her cries,
and unnerves the tiny hummingbird that flies,
abandoning its delicate nest that shakes.

Out on the horizon of pasture grass,
where the mist evaporates, the arrows of dawn
announce that full daylight is coming on
and in the distance bulls and stallions pass,

running fast, happy, their eyes wide,
their manes shaggy, the wind whipping their tails.
Their hoof beats resound, their nostrils, as each inhales,
flare, and flecks of foam fly out to to the side.

Les caïmans, le long des berges embusqués,
Guettent, en soulevant du dos la vase noire,
Le jaguar qui descend au fleuve pour y boire
Et qui hume dans l'air leurs effluves musqués.

Mais sur l'îlot moussu que la rosée imbibe,
Par les vagues rumeurs troublé dans son sommeil,
Se déroule, haussant sa spirale au soleil,
Le vieux roi des pythons, l'Aboma caraïbe.

La mâle torsion de ses muscles d'acier
Soutient le col superbe et la tête squameuse;
Sa queue en longs frissons fouette l'onde écumeuse;
Il se dresse du haut de son orgueil princier.

Armuré de topaze et casqué d'émeraude,
Comme une idole antique immobile en ses noeuds,
Tel, baigné de lumière, il rêve, dédaigneux
Et splendide, et dardant sa prunelle qui rôde.

Puis, quand l'ardeur céleste enveloppe à la fois
Les nappes d'eau torride et la terre enflammée,
Il plonge, et va chercher sa proie accoutumée,
Le taureau, le jaguar, ou l'homme, au fond des bois.

The crocodiles along the riverbank
watch. Only their eyes are not submersed.
The jaguar now descends to quench his thirst
and the air, touched by his scent, is musky and rank.

But out on the island nestled in his bed
of moss, roused from his drowse by this bruit,
the Aboma, the king of pythons, languidly
uncoils his spiral and rears his gorgeous head.

The animal's muscles that seem to be made of steel
arch his neck and allow the light to play
on his lovely scales he seems to like to display.
It rears higher in the pride that princes feel.

Topaz and emerald gleam from his armor. Like
an ancient idol still in its temple niche
he is bathed in light and he dreams extravagant rich
visions. His eyes dart. He is ready to strike.

In time, when heaven's heat comes beating upon
the river water as well as the earth, he dives
in and goes after prey. Nothing survives—
neither strong bull, quick jaguar, nor man.

LE VENT FROID DE LA NUIT

Le vent froid de la nuit souffle à travers les branches
Et casse par moments les rameaux desséchés;
La neige, sur la plaine où les morts sont couchés,
Comme un suaire étend au loin ses nappes blanches.

En ligne noire, au bord de l'étroit horizon,
Un long vol de corbeaux passe en rasant la terre,
Et quelques chiens, creusant un tertre solitaire,
Entre-choquent les os dans le rude gazon.

J'entends gémir les morts sous les herbes froissées.
Ô pâles habitants de la nuit sans réveil,
Quel amer souvenir, troublant votre sommeil,
S'échappe en lourds sanglots de vos lèvres glacées?

Oubliez, oubliez! Vos coeurs sont consumés;
De sang et de chaleur vos artères sont vides.
Ô morts, morts bienheureux, en proie aux vers avides,
Souvenez-vous plutôt de la vie, et dormez!

Ah! dans vos lits profonds quand je pourrai descendre,
Comme un forçat vieilli qui voit tomber ses fers,
Que j'aimerai sentir, libre des maux soufferts,
Ce qui fut moi rentrer dans la commune cendre!

Mais, ô songe! Les morts se taisent dans leur nuit.
C'est le vent, c'est l'effort des chiens à leur pâture,
C'est ton morne soupir, implacable nature!
C'est mon coeur ulcéré qui pleure et qui gémit.

THE COLD NIGHT WIND

The cold night wind blows through the bare trees,
sometimes breaking branches that are dry;
snow covers the plain where the dead lie
like a tablecloth in improvised obsequies.

In a black line on the narrow horizon, crows
go skimming in formation close to the ground,
and a pack of dogs is digging into a mound
for buried bones they are eager to expose.

I hear a moaning arise from the dead grass.
O denizens of the night-time, do not wake!
Your memories and painful dreams will take
their toll and you will sob again, Alas!

Forget it, forget it all! Your hearts are still.
Your arteries are empty of blood and heat.
For the fortunate dead, oblivion is sweet
without any trace of pain, desire, or will.

Deep in your graves you can rest easy, and I
envy you, old convicts whose fetters fall,
free of the evils that you have suffered, all
consumed in the pyre, their cinders drifting high.

The dead are resting silently now in their
sleep. In the wind are dogs digging for food,
and implacable nature driving us all. I would
weep for us and the sufferings we bear.

Tais-toi. Le ciel est sourd, la terre te dédaigne.
À quoi bon tant de pleurs si tu ne peux guérir?
Sois comme un loup blessé qui se tait pour mourir,
Et qui mord le couteau, de sa gueule qui saigne.

Encore une torture, encore un battement.
Puis, rien. La terre s'ouvre, un peu de chair y tombe;
Et l'herbe de l'oubli, cachant bientôt la tombe,
Sur tant de vanité croît éternellement.

But what's the point? The exigencies of life
are not worth tears if one cannot rectify
the world. The wounded wolf knows he must die
and with his bleeding mouth bites at the knife.

Torture and more torture, blows, and then
nothing, nothing. Earth opens its jaws
and swallows our flesh. Without the slightest pause,
grass grows over the vanity of men.

PAYSAGE POLAIRE

Un monde mort, immense écume de la mer,
Gouffre d'ombre stérile et de lueurs spectrales,
Jets de pics convulsifs étirés en spirales
Qui vont éperdument dans le brouillard amer.

Un ciel rugueux, roulant par blocs, un âpre enfer,
Où passent à plein vol les clameurs sépulcrales,
Les rires, les sanglots, les cris aigus, les râles
Qu'un vent sinistre arrache à son clairon de fer.

Sur les hauts caps branlants, rongés des flots voraces,
Se roidissent les Dieux brumeux des vieilles races,
Congelés dans leur rêve et leur lividité;

Et les grands ours, blanchis par les neiges antiques,
çà et là, balançant leurs cous épileptiques,
Ivres et monstrueux, bavent de volupté.

POLAR LANDSCAPE

A dead world of frozen sea-spume, stark,
sterile, and cold, but with odd glints of light
of a spectral kind that disturb the endless night
and show the fog-bound mountains, distant and dark.

The wind howls in sepulchral tones that can sound
like laughter or tears, or screams or dismal groans,
but then subsides to a series of drawn-out moans
that complain to the sky as they rise up from the ground.

From the mountain peaks that look like frozen waves,
the old gods look down as if on the graves
of civilizations of which they dream at night,

while a great bear crosses the ancient snows,
stretching his neck, lumbering as he goes
as a drunk might, and drooling with delight.

L'OASIS

Derrière les coteaux stériles de Kobbé
Comme un bloc rouge et lourd le soleil est tombé;
Un vol de vautours passe et semble le poursuivre.
Le ciel terne est rayé de nuages de cuivre;
Et de sombres lueurs, vers l'Est, traînent encor,
Pareilles aux lambeaux de quelque robe d'or.
Le rugueux Sennaar, jonché de pierres rousses
Qui hérissent le sable ou déchirent les mousses,
A travers la vapeur de ses marais malsains
Ondule jusqu'au pied des versants Abyssins.
La nuit tombe. On entend les koukals aux cris aigres.
Les hyènes, secouant le poil de leurs dos maigres,
De buissons en buissons se glissent en râlant.
L'hippopotame souffle aux berges du Nil blanc
Et vautre, dans les joncs rigides qu'il écrase,
Son ventre rose et gras tout cuirassé de vase.
Autour des flaques d'eau saumâtre où les chakals
Par bandes viennent boire, en longeant les nopals,
L'aigu fourmillement des stridentes bigaylles
S'épaissit et tournoie au-dessus des broussailles;
Tandis que, du désert en Nubie emporté,
Un vent âcre, chargé de chaude humidité,
Avec une rumeur vague et sinistre, agite
Les rudes palmiers-doums où l'ibis fait son gîte.
Voici ton heure, ô roi du Sennaar, ô chef
Dont le soleil endort le rugissement bref.
Sous la roche concave et pleine d'os qui luisent,
Contre l'âpre granit tes ongles durs s'aiguisent.
Arquant tes souples reins fatigués du repos,
Et ta crinière jaune éparse sur le dos,
Tu te lèves, tu viens d'un pas mélancolique

THE OASIS

Behind the dry and barren hills of Kobbé
the sun is like a brick at the end of the day,
heavy and red and falling. Overhead
a vulture cruises for anything dying or dead
to feast on. The sky is a coppery color but there
is shredding as on a hem the worse for wear
of a gold ball gown. The rough Sennar is strewn
with rocks as if on the surface of the moon.
With their sickly miasma the marshes extend as far
as the Abyssinian border where there are
the foothills and then real mountains. Night is falling
and with their *goop-goop-goop* the Koukals are calling.
Scrawny hyenas dart from the bushes while
the hippopotami snort in the White Nile,
wallow in the water, and trample down
the rushes. Their pink bellies are splotched with brown
river mud. Cautiously at the brink
of the water a band of jackals comes to drink
the brackish water under the nopal trees
where strident bigaylles call incivilities
that further thicken the heavy atmosphere
afflicted by Nubian winds that deposit here
their heat. The doum-palms rustle, and this is
a cause for concern for their resident ibises.
This is your hour, O king of Semmar, great chief,
when the burning sun quiets the roar for a brief
moment at least. Under your concave
rock where you doze among the bones you have
gnawed clean, you sharpen your curved claws
on the granite face, and stretch, and lick your paws.
You take a somber step or two and stare

Aspirer l'air du soir sur ton seuil famélique,
Et, le front haut, les yeux à l'horizon dormant,
Tu regardes l'espace et rugis sourdement.
Sur la lividité du ciel la lune froide
De la proche oasis découpe l'ombre roide,
Où, las d'avoir marché par les terrains bourbeux,
Les hommes du Darfour font halte avec leurs boeufs.
Ils sont couchés là-bas auprès de la citerne
Dont un rayon de lune argente l'onde terne.
Les uns, ayant mangé le mil et le maïs,
S'endorment en parlant du retour au pays;
Ceux-ci, pleins de langueur, rêvant de grasses herbes,
Et le mufle enfoui dans leurs fanons superbes,
Ruminent lentement sur leur lit de graviers.
À toi la chair des boeufs ou la chair des bouviers!
Le vent a consumé leurs feux de ronce sèche;
Ta narine s'emplit d'une odeur vive et fraîche,
Ton ventre bat, la faim hérisse tes cheveux,
Et tu plonges dans l'ombre en quelques bonds nerveux.

at all that space. You sniff the evening air.
The livid sky silvered by moonlight seems
ominous as in some disturbing dreams.
But you are hungry. Near the oasis, you know
that men of Darfur, wearied by their slow
journey home, have stopped to rest for the night,
pitch their camp in what is left of the light,
drink water and eat handfuls of millet or maize,
water the weary cattle, and let them graze.
They talk of home to stay awake and keep
watch over the herd. A few of them sleep,
as the cows do too, dreaming of lush grass,
unaware that the slightest breezes that pass
brings the lion the news of bovine flesh
and human, too. His nostrils note the fresh
scent, and his pang of hunger ruffles his mane.
While his tawny belly quivers slightly, his brain
is steady as he rouses himself to leap
into the nervous landscape, black and deep.

LA VIPÈRE

Si les chastes amours avec respect louées
Éblouissent encor ta pensée et tes yeux,
N'effleure point les plis de leurs robes nouées,
Garde la pureté de ton rêve pieux.
Ces blanches visions, ces vierges que tu crées
Sont ta jeunesse en fleur épanouie au ciel !
Verse à leurs pieds le flot de tes larmes sacrées,
Brûle tous tes parfums sur leur mystique autel.

Mais si l'amer venin est entré dans tes veines,
Pâle de volupté pleurée et de langueur,
Tu chercheras en vain un remède à tes peines :
L'angoisse du néant te remplira le cœur.
Ployé sous ton fardeau de honte et de misère,
D'un exécrable mal ne vis pas consumé :
Arrache de ton sein la mortelle vipère,
Ou tais-toi, lâche, et meurs, meurs d'avoir trop aimé !

THE VIPER

In those chaste dreams of love that filled your mind
once and dazzled your eyes with visions of white
robes and endless processions of virgins, refined
but beautiful, before you every night,
remember that you created them behind
closed lids, oneiric creatures, the blossoms of your
innocence and youth. Such tears as you might
have shed for them, you won't shed anymore.

The viper strikes: its venom enters your veins,
and you fall sick, feel languid, and you try
to find some cure. You wrack your addled brains,
but your shame and misery interact. You sigh
in the anguish that the poison has brought on
and that festers in your chest where the viper bit.
That healthy innocence you had is gone
and the death you fear is the only cure for it.

BERNICA

Perdu sur la montagne, entre deux parois hautes,
Il est un lieu sauvage, au rêve hospitalier,
Qui, dès le premier jour, n'a connu que peu d'hôtes;
Le bruit n'y monte pas de la mer sur les côtes,
Ni la rumeur de l'homme : on y peut oublier.

La liane y suspend dans l'air ses belles cloches
Où les frelons, gorgés de miel, dorment blottis;
Un rideau d'aloès en défend les approches;
Et l'eau vive qui germe aux fissures des roches
Y fait tinter l'écho de son clair cliquetis.

Quand l'aube jette aux monts sa rose bandelette,
Cet étroit paradis, parfumé de verdeurs,
Au-devant du soleil, comme une cassolette,
Enroule autour des pics la brume violette
Qui, par frais tourbillons, sort de ses profondeurs.

Si Midi, du ciel pur, verse sa lave blanche,
Au travers des massifs il n'en laisse pleuvoir
Que des éclats légers qui vont, de branche en branche,
Fluides diamants que l'une à l'autre épanche,
De leurs taches de feu semer le gazon noir.

Parfois, hors des fourrés, les oreilles ouvertes,
L'oeil au guet, le col droit, et la rosée au flanc,
Un cabri voyageur, en quelques bonds alertes,
Vient boire aux cavités pleines de feuilles vertes,
Les quatre pieds posés sur un caillou tremblant.

BERNICA

Hidden away in the mountains between two sheer
cliffs is a wild but hospitable retreat
from the busy world. There are no visitors here,
or any human noises. In this clear
air is primeval silence, pure, complete.

Lianas hang in the air with delicate bell-
like flowers where the huddled hornets doze,
drunk either with honey or just the smell
of the blossoms. A curtain of aloe protects well
from strangers a place that only the native knows.

The considerate dawn arranges a rosy shawl
upon the mountain's shoulders in this sublime
sample of paradise, perfect but small,
and subtle perfumes arise from flowers of all
colors and shapes to mix with the haze and climb

to the highest peaks. To the south from a clear sky
torrents rain down, but the mountain range protects
the valley from such showers, although on high
occasional lightning flashes intensify
the branches on which each drop of water reflects

the light as brightly as diamonds would. But see,
a kid appears, ears pricked, to drink from the springs.
or the mossy hollows in the rock ledge. He
has found a foothold and stands tremblingly
for a only moment and then, as if he had wings,

Tout un essaim d'oiseaux fourmille, vole et rôde
De l'arbre aux rocs moussus, et des herbes aux fleurs:
Ceux-ci trempent dans l'eau leur poitrail d'émeraude;
Ceux-là, séchant leur plume à la brise plus chaude,
Se lustrent d'un bec frêle aux bords des nids siffleurs.

Ce sont des chœurs soudains, des chansons infinies,
Un long gazouillement d'appels joyeux mêlé,
Ou des plaintes d'amour à des rires unies;
Et si douces, pourtant, flottent ces harmonies,
Que le repos de l'air n'en est jamais troublé.

Mais l'âme s'en pénètre; elle se plonge, entière,
Dans l'heureuse beauté de ce monde charmant;
Elle se sent oiseau, fleur, eau vive et lumière;
Elle revêt ta robe, ô pureté première!
Et se repose en Dieu silencieusement.

is gone. But swarms of insects and birds abide
to animate the prospect. They dart or hover
above bejeweled grasses, soar and glide,
or perch and rest until their wings are dried.
Look sharp and in its nest you can spot a plover.

Everywhere the songs of birds resound,
expressions of simple joy, or else laments
for loves that are more easily lost than found.
These floating harmonies one hears all around
fall silent for a while and recommence.

They seize my soul, transporting me to a new
level of happiness. Beauty such as this
with the birds, the flowers, the sunlight on the dew,
the purity I see and I see through
is God's display of a splendor that is His.

LE COLIBRI

Le vert colibri, le roi des collines,
Voyant la rosée et le soleil clair
Luire dans son nid tissé d'herbes fines,
Comme un frais rayon s'échappe dans l'air.

Il se hâte et vole aux sources voisines
Où les bambous font le bruit de la mer,
Où l'açoka rouge, aux odeurs divines,
S'ouvre et porte au coeur un humide éclair.

Vers la fleur dorée il descend, se pose,
Et boit tant d'amour dans la coupe rose,
Qu'il meurt, ne sachant s'il l'a pu tarir.

Sur ta lèvre pure, ô ma bien-aimée,
Telle aussi mon âme eût voulu mourir
Du premier baiser qui l'a parfumée!

THE HUMMINGBIRD

The green hummingbird, king of the hills, sees
the glisten of morning dew and the sun's bright light
on the nest he has woven high up in the trees,
and he rises up like a spark to vanish from sight.

He darts at once toward the nearby spring, a mise-
en-scène of bamboo in which even a slight
breeze rustles the grove with a sound like the sea's,
and the red hibiscus blossoms guide his flight.

From these he sips the sweet liqueurs of his
passion to surfeit and more, for his life is
far too short to satisfy his craving—

as on your rosebud lips where often I
have drunk thirsty for more of what I was having,
my greedy soul both feared and longed to die.

LE MANCHY

Sous un nuage frais de claire mousseline,
    Tous les dimanches au matin,
Tu venais à la ville en manchy de rotin,
    Par les rampes de la colline.

La cloche de l'église alertement tintait
    Le vent de mer berçait les cannes
Comme une grêle d'or, aux pointes des savanes,
    Le feu du soleil crépitait.

Le bracelet aux poings, l'anneau sur la cheville,
    Et le mouchoir jaune aux chignons,
Deux telingas portaient, assidus compagnons,
    Ton lit aux nattes de Manille.

Ployant leur jarret maigre et nerveux, et chantant,
    Souples dans leurs tuniques blanches,
Le bambou sur l'épaule et les mains sur les hanches,
    Ils allaient le long de l'Étang.

Le long de la chaussée et des varangues basses
    Où les vieux créoles fumaient,
Par les groupes joyeux des Noirs, ils s'animaient
    Au bruit des bobres Madécasses.

Dans l'air léger flottait l'odeur des tamarins;
    Sur les houles illuminées,
Au large, les oiseaux, en d'immenses traînées,
    Plongeaient dans les brouillards marins..

THE PALANQUIN

Under a gauzy cloud of muslin, you
    appeared on Sundays on your way in-
to the city in your rattan palanquin
    and came up the hill and into view.

The sun showered the day with gold; the sea-
    breezes rustled the canes in the field;
and high in the whitewashed steeple, church bells pealed
    for noon and for you in equal degree.

I can see your bracelet glitter and ankle ring
    and your chignon's bright yellow tie.
Your two Telinga bearers held you high
    on your Manila mat. They'd sing

together as they jogged. With their long stride
    and the bamboo poles on their shoulders and hands
on their hips, they had a certain elegance
    in which each of them seemed to take pride.

Their matching tunics were dazzling white and they
    took the path by the water's edge
where there was a narrow track that ran through the sedge.
    The happy Creoles would play

on their crude Madagascar bobres pleasing
    tunes that filled the tamarind-scented
air. How could anyone not be contented,
    watching the sea-birds diving and seizing

Et tandis que ton pied, sorti de la babouche,
    Pendait, rose, au bord du manchy,
A l'ombre des Bois-Noirs touffus et du Letchi
    Aux fruits moins pourprés que ta bouche;

Tandis qu'un papillon, les deux ailes en fleur,
    Teinté d'azur et d'écarlate,
Se posait par instants sur ta peau délicate
    En y laissant de sa couleur;

On voyait, au travers du rideau de batiste,
    Tes boucles dorer l'oreiller,
Et, sous leurs cils mi-clos, feignant de sommeiller,
    Tes beaux yeux de sombre améthyste.

Tu t'en venais ainsi, par les matins si doux,
    De la montagne à la grand'messe,
Dans ta grâce naïve et ta rose jeunesse,
    Au pas rythmé de tes Hindous.

Maintenant, dans le sable aride de nos grèves,
    Sous les chiendents, au bruit des mers,
Tu reposes parmi les morts qui me sont chers,
    Ô charme de mes premiers rêves!

dainty morsels? Your slender slippered foot
	protruded from the palanquin and made
an accent in sweet pink in the dull shade
	of the trees heavy with litchi fruit.

And there was a pair of delicate red and blue
	butterflies that fluttered in
the breeze or posed for an instant upon your skin
	as yet another embellishment you

hardly required, posed that way with your hair
	spread out upon your pillow as
your eyelids closed in a feigning of sleep that was
	a restful refuge from the sun's glare.

The delicate mountain morning you improved
	by your so graceful passage through it,
your palanquin lending a distinction to it
	as your rhythmic Hindus moved.

Years later walking on this strand I can see
	beyond its dismal, weed-scattered shore
and the crashing waves, your apparition before
	me still—as it will always be.

LES ÉLÉPHANTS

Le sable rouge est comme une mer sans limite,
Et qui flambe, muette, affaissée en son lit.
Une ondulation immobile remplit
L'horizon aux vapeurs de cuivre où l'homme habite.

Nulle vie et nul bruit. Tous les lions repus
Dorment au fond de l'antre éloigné de cent lieues;
Et la girafe boit dans les fontaines bleues,
Là-bas, sous les dattiers des panthères connus.

Pas un oiseau ne passe en fouettant de son aile
L'air épais ou circule un immense soleil.
Parfois quelque boa, chauffé dans son sommeil,
Fait onduler son dos où l'écaille étincelle.

Tel l'espace enflammé brûlé sous les cieux clairs,
Mais, tandis que tout dort aux mornes solitudes,
Les éléphants rugueux, voyageurs lents et rudes,
Vont au pays natal à travers les déserts.

D'un point de l'horizon, comme des masses brunes,
Ils viennent, soulevant la poussière, et l'on voit,
Pour ne point dévier du chemin le plus droit,
Sous leur pied large et sur crouler au loin les dunes.

Celui qui tient la tête est un vieux chef. Son corps
Est gercé comme un tronc que le temps ronge et mine;
Sa tête est comme un roc et l'arc de son échine
Se voûte puissamment à ses moindres efforts.

ELEPHANTS

The red sand stretches out like an endless sea,
mute in its bed, shimmering in the heat,
with its rippled dunes, immobile and complete.
Far out at the horizon, humanity

huddles. Soundless, lifeless—but lions sleep
in a cool cave a hundred leagues away,
where giraffes drink from oasis waters that play,
and panthers, underneath the date palms keep

their vigils. Here no bird's wing stirs the air
congealing beneath the huge sun, under which
a scaly boa dozing in that glare
sometimes shows she's alive by a muscle twitch.

While nothing in that empty wilderness seems
to move beneath the pellucid sky, a herd
of elephants materializes that dreams
of home somewhere to the south. Course and absurd,

they cross the sand, brown mountains raising a cloud
of dust as they move in a straight line and with huge
feet crumble the dunes. Indifferent, proud,
they plod through the shimmer toward their cool refuge.

The one in front is the leader, wrinkled and old
with time's hachure all over his skin. Some trees
have bark like that. He does not have to hold
the others in line behind him, for all of these

Sans ralentir jamais et sans hâter sa marche,
Il guide au but certain ses compagnons poudreux
Et, creusant par derrière un sillon sablonneux,
Les pèlerins massifs suivent leur patriarche.

L'oreille en éventail, la trompe entre les dents,
Ils cheminent, l'oeil clos. Leur ventre bat et fume,
Et leur sueur dans l'air embrasé monte en brume,
Et bourdonnent autour mille insectes ardents.

Mais qu'importent la soif et la mouche vorace,
Et le soleil cuisant leur dos noir et plissé?
Ils rêvent en marchant du pays délaissé,
Des forêts de figuiers où s'abrita leur race.

Ils reverront le fleuve échappé des grands monts,
Ou nage en mugissant l'hippopotame énorme,
Où, blanchis par la lune et projetant leur forme,
Ils descendaient pour boire en écrasant les joncs.

Aussi, pleins de courage et de lenteur, ils passent
Comme une ligne noire, au sable illimité;
Et le désert reprend son immobilité
Quand les lourds voyageurs à l'horizon s'effacent.

creatures know that he knows where they are going.
He makes a path for them and all these dark
beasts trudge along, not hurrying or slowing
like pilgrims in the train of some patriarch.

Their ears fanned out, their trunks swaying between
their swooping tusks, they follow with their eyes
shut. Their sweat gives their bodies a sheen
and also attracts thousands of gnats and flies

that swarm about them, but they don't seem to care.
Their goal is to see again their verdant home
as empty as this but with fig trees everywhere
and wide brownish rivers that wind down from

distant mountains in which hippos swim,
roaring sometimes. In the silvery moonlight their gray
bulks will trample the rushes and their dim
shapes crowd at the bank to drink and spray

themselves and one another. Brave and slow
they cross the distant horizon and disappear,
leaving the sand's emptiness as though
no great beasts like them were ever here.

LA MORT D'UN LION

Étant un vieux chasseur altéré de grand air
Et du sang noir des boeufs, il avait l'habitude
De contempler de haut les plaines et la mer,
Et de rugir en paix, libre en sa solitude.

Aussi, comme un damné qui rôde dans l'enfer,
Pour l'inepte plaisir de cette multitude
Il allait et venait dans sa cage de fer,
Heurtant les deux cloisons avec sa tête rude.

L'horrible sort, enfin, ne devant plus changer,
Il cessa brusquement de boire et de manger,
Et la mort emporta son âme vagabonde.

Ô coeur toujours en proie à la rébellion,
Qui tournes, haletant, dans la cage du monde,
Lâche, que ne fais-tu comme a fait ce lion?

DEATH OF A LION

A tired hunter on a flat rock in the heat
of the glaring sun can still taste the blood that he
lapped from the bellowing ox as it poured from the meat.
He roars, yawns, and stares out in peace at the sea.

But then, like some soul in hell, he paces instead
in a narrow cage for the crowd's vulgar delight,
running sometimes at the wall to bang his head
against it like some hopeless Bedlamite.

When that fails to accomplish his purpose, the beast
stops eating and drinking: it's slow but at least
reliable. And death takes his vagabond soul.

O proud, rebellious heart that would not be
confined in the cage of a filthy world! His goal
you cannot imagine, coward, less noble than he.

LES RÊVES MORTS

Vois ! cette mer si calme a comme un lourd bélier
Effondré tout un jour le flanc des promontoires,
Escaladé par bonds leur fumant escalier,
Et versé sur les rocs, qui hurlent sans plier,
Le frisson écumeux des longues houles noires.
Un vent frais, aujourd'hui, palpite sur les eaux,
La beauté du soleil monte et les illumine,
Et vers l'horizon pur où nagent les vaisseaux,
De la côte azurée, un tourbillon d'oiseaux
S'échappe, en arpentant l'immensité divine.
Mais, parmi les varechs, aux pointes des îlots,
Ceux qu'a brisés l'assaut sans frein de la tourmente,
Livides et sanglants sous la lourdeur des flots,
La bouche ouverte et pleine encore de sanglots,
Dardent leurs yeux hagards à travers l'eau dormante.
Ami, ton coeur profond est tel que cette mer
Qui sur le sable fin déroule ses volutes :
Il a pleuré, rugi comme l'abîme amer,
Il s'est rué cent fois contre des rocs de fer,
Tout un long jour d'ivresse et d'effroyables luttes.
Maintenant il reflue, il s'apaise, il s'abat.
Sans peur et sans désir que l'ouragan renaisse,
Sous l'immortel soleil c'est à peine s'il bat;
Mais génie, espérance, amour, force et jeunesse
Sont là, morts, dans l'écume et le sang du combat.

DEAD DREAMS

Look! Like a battering ram, the huge sea
attacked the fragile promontory's flank,
climbing its howling rocks relentlessly
by leaps and bounds to break repeatedly
in frothy waves, rank upon long black rank.
A cool breeze tousled the water; the sun
rose and shone on the glistening stone. Far out
on the water almost at the horizon, one
could make out ships. The sea birds had begun
their search for food, flying slowly about
in lazy circles so that they could see
the shoals of fish darting just below
the surface of the blue immensity
the storm had decorated with debris
of seaweed the island's beaches had let go.
Their beaks were open wide, and the birds cried
as their eyes darted this way and that to peer
at the messy surface of the outgoing tide.
My friend, the grief by which your heart was tried
was as wild and deep as the ocean churning here.
He was drunk all day and a hundred times prepared
to fling himself to the rocks over which he stood
and destroy his body about which he no longer cared.
The sun beat down upon him as he dared
embrace his death and its anodyne of blood.

LES SPECTRES

I

Trois spectres familiers hantent mes heures sombres.
Sans relâche, à jamais, perpétuellement,
Du rêve de ma vie ils traversent les ombres.

Je les regarde avec angoisse et tremblement.
Ils se suivent, muets comme il convient aux âmes,
Et mon coeur se contracte et saigne en les nommant.

Ces magnétiques yeux, plus aigus que des lames,
Me blessent fibre à fibre et filtrent dans ma chair;
La moelle de mes os gèle à leurs mornes flammes.

Sur ces lèvres sans voix éclate un rire amer.
Ils m'entraînent, parmi la ronce et les décombres,
Très loin, par un ciel lourd et terne de l'hiver.

Trois spectres familiers hantent mes heures sombres.

II

Ces spectres! on dirait en vérité des morts,
Tant leur face est livide et leurs mains sont glacées.
Ils vivent cependant : ce sont mes trois remords.

Que ne puis-je tarir le flot de mes pensées,
Et dans l'abîme noir et vengeur de l'oubli
Noyer le souvenir des ivresses passées!

SPECTERS

I

Three specters haunt me in my darkest hour,
relentless familiars that come to me to attend
the dream of my life and from their shadows glower.

I watch in fear and quake as they descend
as mute as the souls of the dead would have to be,
and my heart's blood freezes—as they intend.

Their piercing eyes, sharper than knives, cut me
in muscle, nerve, and the marrow of my bones,
and my body burns in exquisite agony.

On voiceless lips more suitable for moans
there is a derisive laugh of awful power
and then they drag me off among brambles and stones.

Three specters haunt me in my darkest hour.

II

These wraiths, these specters are spirits of the dead,
with their ghastly livid faces and hands of ice.
But they are alive and even high-spirited.

They are regrets, from hell, or paradise,
or oblivion, and they come to punish me
for moments of rapture and extort their exorbitant price.

J'ai brûlé les parfums dont vous m'aviez empli;
Le flambeau s'est éteint sur l'autel en ruines;
Tout, fumée et poussière, est bien enseveli.

Rien ne renaîtra plus de tant de fleurs divines,
Car du rosier céleste, hélas! sans trop d'efforts,
Vous avez bu la sève et tranché les racines.

Ces spectres! on dirait en vérité des morts!

III

Les trois spectres sont là qui dardent leurs prunelles.
Je revois le soleil des paradis perdus!
L'espérance sacrée en chantant bat des ailes.

Et vous, vers qui montaient mes désirs éperdus,
Chères âmes, parlez, je vous ai tant aimées!
Ne me rendrez-vous plus les biens qui me sont dus?

Au nom de cet amour dont vous fûtes charmées,
Laissez comme autrefois rayonner vos beaux yeux;
Déroulez sur mon coeur vos tresses parfumées!

Mais tandis que la nuit lugubre étreint les cieux,
Debout, se détachant de ces brumes mortelles,
Les voici devant moi, blancs et silencieux.

Les trois spectres sont là qui dardent leurs prunelles.

The perfumes you used to use so subtly
have faded away. The torch that used to blaze
has guttered to ash and dust's infinity.

Those flowers can never rise again from the clay's
grip to bloom once more, and be watered and fed.
You have cut the roots of those delightful days.

These wraiths, these specters are spirits of the dead.

III

These three dire specters with glaring eyes…
I remember the sunshine of a paradise lost
when hopes and happiness flourished in our skies.

And you who know the truth of my star-crossed
loves, dear souls, do you speak of them to me
with every moment itemized and glossed?

For the sake of our old loves, just leave me be
with your bright eyes shining as I remember you.
My captive heart has not yet struggled free.

The gloomy night embraces heaven's blue,
while all about me noxious miasmas rise
in a white silence, threatening as they do,

these three dire specters with glaring eyes...

IV

Oui! le dogme terrible, ô mon coeur, a raison.
En vain les songes d'or y versent leurs délices,
Dans la coupe où tu bois nage un secret poison.

Tout homme est revêtu d'invisibles cilices;
Et dans l'enivrement de la félicité
La guêpe du désir ravive nos supplices.

Frémirons-nous toujours sous ce vol irrité?
N'arracherons-nous point ce dard qui nous torture?
Ni dans ce monde, ni dans notre éternité.

La vieille Illusion fait de nous sa pâture;
Nul captif n'atteindra le seuil de sa prison;
Et la guêpe est au sein de l'immense nature.

Oui! le dogme terrible, ô mon coeur, a raison.

IV

The dogma is cruel in which my heart believes
with vain dreams of gold that can buy delight,
for there's poison in the cup that it receives.

Men in invisible sackcloth practice this rite
and are drunk with happiness—at least for a time—
when the wasp of desire inflicts its painful bite.

We quiver like sick men, but our hopes climb
and we attempt to fly, though of course we fall,
after our hopeless attempt to achieve the sublime.

But who can shake the illusion possessing us all?
The prisoner with his glimpse of daylight grieves.
The wasp is huge and we are very small.

The dogma is cruel in which my heart believes.

LA FONTAINE AUX LIANES

Comme le flot des mers ondulant vers les plages,
Ô bois, vous déroulez, pleins d'arome et de nids,
Dans l'air splendide et bleu, vos houles de feuillages;
Vous êtes toujours vieux et toujours rajeunis.

Le temps a respecté, rois aux longues années,
Vos grands fronts couronnés de lianes d'argent;
Nul pied ne foulera vos feuilles non fanées:
Vous verrez passer l'homme et le monde changeant.

Vous inclinez d'en haut, au penchant des ravines,
Vos rameaux lents et lourds qu'ont brûlés les éclairs;
Qu'il est doux, le repos de vos ombres divines,
Aux soupirs de la brise, aux chansons des flots clairs!

Le soleil de midi fait palpiter vos sèves;
Vous siégez, revêtus de sa pourpre, et sans voix;
Mais la nuit, épanchant la rosée et les rêves,
Apaise et fait chanter les âmes et les bois.

Par delà les verdeurs des zones maternelles
Où vous poussez d'un jet vos troncs inébranlés,
Seules, plus près du ciel, les neiges éternelles
Couvrent de leurs plis blancs les pics immaculés.

Ô bois natals, j'errais sous vos larges ramures
L'aube aux flancs noirs des monts marchait d'un pied vermeil;
La mer avec lenteur éveillait ses murmures,
Et de tout oeil vivant fuyait le doux sommeil.

THE VINE-COVERED FOUNTAIN

As the endless waves of the ocean crash on the sands
of beaches, you have your rising up and abating
surges of blue-green leaves that are the land's
waves, ancient and always rejuvenating.

To kings respect is given, and for you
with your crown of silver lianas the protocol
is to keep men from passing idly through,
approaching, or intruding upon you at all.

From above, the dramatic angle of the ravine's
wall displays your floral ornaments
that flashes of lighting show off as in vitrines
of the finest shops with their studied opulence.

The midday sun beats down upon you, dressed
in purple and keeping your silent vigil, and night
pours down its sweet dew and offers rest
and soothing dreams of comfort and delight.

Beyond the green of your youngest and tenderest plants,
your jet of water thrusts up like the trunk
of a liquid tree. Even a casual glance
must follow it upward to distant peaks that are sunk

under their blankets of dazzling white snow,
immaculate above your insistent green
vegetation running riot below,
and offer an otherness lofty, cold, and clean.

Au bord des nids, ouvrant ses ailes longtemps closes,
L'oiseau disait le jour avec un chant plus frais
Que la source agitant les verts buissons de roses,
Que le rire amoureux du vent dans les forêts.

Les abeilles sortaient des ruches naturelles
Et par essaims vibraient au soleil matinal;
Et, livrant le trésor de leurs corolles frêles,
Chaque fleur répandait sa goutte de cristal.

Et le ciel descendait dans les claires rosées
Dont la montagne bleue au loin étincelait;
Un mol encens fumait des plantes arrosées
Vers la sainte nature à qui mon coeur parlait.

Au fond des bois baignés d'une vapeur céleste,
Il était une eau vive où rien ne remuait;
Quelques joncs verts, gardiens de la fontaine agreste,
S'y penchaient au hasard en un groupe muet.

Les larges nénuphars, les lianes errantes,
Blancs archipels, flottaient enlacés sur les eaux,
Et dans leurs profondeurs vives et transparentes
Brillait un autre ciel où nageaient les oiseaux.

Ô fraîcheur des forêts, sérénité première,
Ô vents qui caressiez les feuillages chanteurs,
Fontaine aux flots heureux où jouait la lumière,
Éden épanoui sur les vertes hauteurs!

Salut, ô douce paix, et vous, pures haleines,
Et vous qui descendiez du ciel et des rameaux,
Repos du coeur, oubli de la joie et des peines!
Salut! ô sanctuaire interdit à nos maux!

O native woods, I have wandered among your boughs
as silver-footed dawn approached your somber
mountainside and from its sighing drowse
awakened the nearby sea from its restless slumber.

From the lip of its nest, stretching its wings, a bird
proclaimed the day in iterative phrases
to bless the roses or, if one preferred,
a song of love and joy and worldly praises.

The bees emerged from their hives to give the sunlight
an electric buzz as they flew their familiar round
among the flowers, red and blue and white,
to collect the crystal nectar with which they abound.

The brightening sky at least for the moment turned
pink, and the blue mountain far off shone
like a vivid backdrop. A mist, until it burned
off, watered the flowers. I stood alone

as if in an empty cathedral. The fountain's play
was the only movement. A wall of thick green rushes
surrounded the fountain's elegant display
I'd heard and then managed to glimpse through the bushes.

Water lilies in archipelagos
lay on the water's surface, and small birds drank,
bathed, and splashed, enlivening the tableau's
stillness as they dried themselves on the bank.

O cool primeval forest, a gentle breeze
rustles the leaves of your trees so that they seem
to celebrate the tranquility and ease
of the clearing as if it came from Adam's dream.

Et, sous le dôme épais de la forêt profonde,
Aux réduits du lac bleu dans les bois épanché,
Dormait, enveloppé du suaire de l'onde,
Un mort, les yeux au ciel, sur le sable couché.

Il ne sommeillait pas, calme comme Ophélie,
Et souriant comme elle, et les bras sur le sein;
Il était de ces morts que bientôt on oublie;
Pâle et triste, il songeait au fond du clair bassin.

La tête au dur regard reposait sur la pierre;
Aux replis de la joue où le sable brillait,
On eût dit que des pleurs tombaient de la paupière
Et que le coeur encor par instants tressaillait.

Sur les lèvres errait la sombre inquiétude.
Immobile, attentif, il semblait écouter
Si quelque pas humain, troublant la solitude,
De son suprême asile allait le rejeter.

Jeune homme, qui choisis pour ta couche azurée
La fontaine des bois aux flots silencieux,
Nul ne sait la liqueur qui te fut mesurée
Au calice éternel des esprits soucieux.

De quelles passions la jeunesse assaillie
Vint-elle ici chercher le repos dans la mort?
Ton âme à son départ ne fut pas recueillie,
Et la vie a laissé sur ton front un remord.

Pourquoi jusqu'au tombeau cette tristesse amère?
Ce coeur s'est-il brisé pour avoir trop aimé?
La blanche illusion, l'espérance éphémère
En s'envolant au ciel l'ont-elles vu fermé?

Greetings to you, sweet peace and temperate air
that spill down from heaven through the canopy
of foliage, healing hope as well as despair
in this sanctuary of tranquility.

But beneath the forest's overarching dome
the clearing approximates, as if asleep,
a body that was laid out as if on some
catafalque while the waves of the ocean keep

their mournful, whispering vigil. His body lay
less peacefully than Ophelia's did with her sweet
smile and her hands crossed on her breast to pray,
but pale, sad, and bitter in his defeat.

The head, its eyes still open, rested upon
a stone; in the delicate folds of its cheek there seemed
to be a shining track of tears that had run
down his face from the eyelids and still gleamed.

But was the body trembling now and then?
The downward curve of the lips that he affected
bespoke distress: beyond the world of men,
had he longed for peace and rest but been rejected?

Young man, you chose for your cere-cloth this azure
sky, and for your sepulcher this grove.
What chalice were you given and what liqueur
by the worried spirits who saw that you were in love?

What strong passions could have attacked your youth
and driven you here to seek repose in dying?
Your soul was unprepared to concede the truth
of love and writhes in a shame beyond all sighing.

Tu n'es pas né sans doute au bord des mers dorées,
Et tu n'as pas grandi sous les divins palmiers;
Mais l'avare soleil des lointaines contrées
N'a pas mûri la fleur de tes songes premiers.

À l'heure où de ton sein la flamme fut ravie,
Ô jeune homme qui vins dormir en ces beaux lieux,
Une image divine et toujours poursuivie,
Un ciel mélancolique ont passé dans tes yeux.

Si ton âme ici-bas n'a point brisé sa chaîne,
Si la source au flot pur n'a point lavé tes pleurs,
Si tu ne peux partir pour l'étoile prochaine,
Reste, épuise la vie et tes chères douleurs!

Puis, ô pâle étranger, dans ta fosse bleuâtre,
Libre des maux soufferts et d'une ombre voilé,
Que la nature au moins ne te soit point marâtre!
Repose entre ses bras, paisible et consolé.

Tel je songeais. Les bois, sous leur ombre odorante,
Épanchant un concert que rien ne peut tarir,
Sans m'écouter, berçaient leur gloire indifférente,
Ignorant que l'on souffre et qu'on puisse en mourir.

La fontaine limpide, en sa splendeur native,
Réfléchissait toujours les cieux de flamme emplis,
Et sur ce triste front nulle haleine plaintive
De flots riants et purs ne vint rider les plis.

Sur les blancs nénuphars l'oiseau ployant ses ailes
Buvait de son bec rose en ce bassin charmant
Et, sans penser aux morts, tout couvert d'étincelles,
Volait sécher sa plume au tiède firmament.

How did this bitter sorrow bring you to
the grave? How did it break your loving heart?
Your hopes flew high and flashed across the blue
sky for an instant only to depart,

leaving you in black despair. Your days
did not commence on the shores of these golden seas
or under our palm trees, and the sun's rays
do not elsewhere produce such flowers as these.

It was here that the flame in your breast was first ignited,
poor youth, who came here to this paradise
with its striking beauty that ought to have delighted
you, had your pained soul not closed your eyes.

Until your soul's earthly fetters are
broken and the tears are washed from your blind
eyes, you cannot depart to the next star.
Rest, then, leaving life and its pains behind.

Then, in the pit where you lie, a ghastly blue
corpse, free of all pain, the shadows gone,
you'll return to mother nature who cradles you
tenderly now in her arms to comfort her son.

Or so I hope. The trees, meanwhile, produce
their rich and fragrant shade that you and I
enjoy but find depressing, mortals whose
lot it is to suffer and then to die.

In innocence, the crystal fountain reflects
a bright sun in the sky that will always shine.
No end of grief or human complaint corrects
the certainty of the fountain or the vine.

La nature se rit des souffrances humaines;
Ne contemplant jamais que sa propre grandeur,
Elle dispense à tous ses forces souveraines
Et garde pour sa part le calme et la splendeur.

Skimming the white lilies, birds on the wing
dip their beaks in the basin and flutter away
in the joy of their being. And none of them would think,
as their feathers dry, of the dead youth on display.

Nature is not sentimental: it ignores
the sorry plight of men, occupied with its own
grandeurs of which it is the sovereign and source,
and in its majesty enjoys alone.

ABOUT THE TRANSLATOR

DAVID R. SLAVITT was born in White Plains, New York. He earned a BA in 1956 from Yale, graduating magna cum laude, and an MA from Columbia in 1957. He has since authored more than one hundred books of poetry, literary fiction, pulp fiction, memoir, criticism, and translation. He has translated text from Latin, Greek, Hebrew, Greenlandic, French, Italian, and Spanish, including *The Metamorphoses of Ovid* and *The Book of the Twelve Prophets*, as well as works by Sophocles, Horace, Seneca, Dante, Boethius, Marie de France, and others. Slavitt is the recipient of numerous awards, including a National Endowment for the Arts fellowship for translation, an award for literature from the American Academy and Institute of Arts and Letters, and a Rockefeller Foundation artist's residency. He lives in Cambridge, Massachusetts.